Tool kit

For

Children

For living their best life

Tool kit for Children

For living their best life

by

AMIT MEHTA

amBOOKS

Dear child

The day you came

The Sun shone brighter

You looked so pretty

& Yet like a fighter

O Yes, I remember those eyes

Glaring straight at me

For the very first time

they looked at me

As if they were mine!

---- A parent who cares

For that indescribable feeling.......

Picture credit: jakobking85-pixabay.com

Contents

Author's Note

Written words are better than speech due to their holding value. They can be preserved and can be referred back to, as many times as one wishes.

Speech can be effective too but more often is not comprehensive, is unorganized and lacks the grasping power.

The listener can, more often than not, get immersed in self-thoughts, can get distracted and may seem outwardly attentive.

The content can get lost by distraction.

Also, to say it all in one sitting does not seem viable and a second session breaks the context of the first.

So, I am writing this down for you, Children.

This book has essential tools with my observations, even experiences from my own life.

The topics almost came out one after the other and all seem very practical and relevant.

They can be referred to at any point, even later in life. Everyone has unique experiences but the underlying current of these topics would be somewhat similar and might help!

In the real world, when children step out of the comforts of their homes, away from parents, and grandparents, they almost suddenly start to get these bouncers thrown at them.

Siddharth Gautam, later known as **"Buddha", the enlightened One**, was gravely overwhelmed when he came out on the street, from the confinement of his comforts.

So much so that he became deeply depressed seeing so much misery, the kind he had not even heard of, leave aside experienced any.

Dear Parent,

Yes, life can be truly overwhelming and it seems almost critical to prepare your child with what all she or he can come across for a better confrontation and a smoother transition!

I hope this book will help you as much as it does to anyone who wants a customized tool kit to pass on to their children for their journey...

Though, they will still have to scale the mountain themselves, face the storms alone, soak in the brilliant sunshine, and appreciate the Sunflowers along the way!

No guide or book or tool kit can match up to it.

Dear Children,

NO ONE CAN STEAL YOUR THUNDER FROM YOU.

THE THUNDER OF LOVE, COURAGE, HAPPINESS, ADVENTURE & LIFE.

This book is the only tool kit you will find in order to live your best life.

Read it with full honesty & pure intent.

There are powerful insights that will get rooted in your subconscious mind & will appear whenever you need them, at the right time, just like a true friend.

This is a treasure you have stumbled upon! Grab it with both your hands & enjoy its riches!

<u>**MY EARNEST REQUEST TO CHILDREN & PARENTS**</u>

This book is as relevant for an eight-year-old child as it is for a fifteen year one, or even a student entering college or passing out.

In fact, the earlier a child can be handed over these tools, the more beneficial will it be to better prepare them for the challenges of life and to provide a basic framework of the real life early on!

For younger children the parents have to contribute with their time & care, to recite these lessons, slowly and in a language best suited for their children, as all of them are unique and have varied understanding levels. The tools are auto-tuned to all age group of children!

For children who can now read on their own should study these lessons over and over again until they are deep-rooted. This book will prepare you for life and life is waiting for you with open arms!

While your school & college prepares you for a good career & opportunities, this book prepares you to lead a good life while pursuing your career!

A life where you have a head start over others, as you are already aware of the fundamentals and do not have to figure the same thus saving precious time in your youth.

ALL THE BEST!

Dear children ....

I remember my awe when I first used a Geometry Compass & a Divider or even a wrench and a screwdriver! I was fascinated & amused even before I knew how to use them.

You have a personal Tool kit now. The more you use it, the more it works well.

Keep it with you at all times.

"So, do I mean that by doing all of this, Success is guaranteed?"

(a line from one of the chapters)

The Illusion of Time

Time is made up of seconds, minutes, hours and a day.

While you might think, it is just another monotonous day, one day would have passed, thus pushing your goal ahead by one day.

Time can be deceiving. When you are not doing much, or not in motion, it seems there is a lot of time free with us but when you are in motion and doing lot of things throughout the day, it seems time is flying and that there is so little time!

Time & Motion can form a deception by their inconspicuous nature.

You cannot see time, or touch it or feel it, and hence it is difficult to preserve it or grow it.

Your goal e.g., is to become a designer. So, you project all your energy towards it and imagine yourself on a successful pedestal. We all do that.

Time & Motion

can form a

deception by

their

inconspicuous

nature

No one dreams in isolation, just to live in monotony. We have success and joy in dreams, which motivates us.

We see successful people who made a name for themselves and look up to them. You dream, one day, to become them, like them, or even better.

Now there are two aspects to it.

Either you keep dreaming about all this, be engrossed and engaged thinking about your idols fame, wealth, success, that's one.

Second is to keep this image of success, your image in mind, start to take small steps, every day in this direction.

Slowly and steadily, then you will begin to go near to your goal.

As they say, *"Beginning is half done"*, but only half, mind you!

So, your dream, no matter how boring it may sound, is made up of these common days, simple days, with commoners surrounding you, maybe your parents, friends.

You will have to **Respect your dream & Yourself** and everyday work at it, towards it.

Imagine you aspire to climb the Everest and never taking a step towards it, assuming there is enough time.

It will take years of determination, frustration, hard work, turmoil and fret to be able to make it, but rest assured, it will be a journey worth every drop of your sweat & every blister beneath your feet!

So, do I mean that by doing all of this Success is guaranteed?

When I say that it will all be worth it, do I mean you will realize your dream?

When you dream about scaling the mighty Everest, is there a guarantee that you will reach there?

No.

However, you will still prepare completely and train with utmost passion. Your every pore will be energetic and motivated all the time.

You will lose your sleep and your dream will keep you awake!

You will work harder than your muscles could ever............. your passion & belief will push you every second, every hour, every day.

Respect

your

dream

&

Yourself

You will be happiest thinking about taking the journey and the moment of you reaching to the top will give you goose bumps.

Remember, all this while you will also be aware of the inhuman conditions you will face, the steep, snow-clad hills, the sheer falls at every step, the treacherous next step, which can take you to an eternal obscurity and darkness, hundreds of feet below the ground, never to be found again.

The numerous cunning storms tempting you towards them & promising to devour you all together.

The dark truth about your body misbehaving in those extreme conditions and giving up.

No number of simulations and trainings can prepare you for the real conditions!

And on top of all this you know that many, just like you, dreamt, prepared and lived this dream but succumbed on the way or had to return back, disappointed.

Even after knowing all of this, you still dream, don't you? Is this a foolish thing to do? Is this devoid of all logic?

No!!! it is not.

That's the audacity lof Hope and the beauty of Life!

We don't stop believing in our dream and the pursuit of fulfilling it.

You will notice that even in this example of a time-bound dream of scaling Everest, where the risks are so visible, people still aspire for it.

The dream we talked about in the beginning about becoming a designer or an actor is also achievable but you need to be aware of all the obstacles, pitfalls & roadblocks but still carry on with utmost passion and willpower

It's very easy to look at a masterpiece and aspire to become one, it will be wiser to know that

the Gold, to refine, has gone through more than a thousand degrees Celsius!!

Yes, that much, it's very difficult.

It will break you, to pieces. It will be unbearable at most times, but you need to believe and know that for you to refine, this process is essential.

There will be no shortcuts.

There will be no mercy.

But you will not feel the pain if you are passionately pursuing the journey.......

The Fruit of your perseverance will be Sweet & Tangy.

the Gold,

to refine,

has gone through

more than a

thousand

degree Celsius!!

Most important – even if at the end of your journey you are not able to make it to Everest, you will be much wiser and refined than you were, when you began!

Every milestone you covered added a layer of strength and wisdom, never forget this.

You have not failed if you met with a different outcome, you have become better, to try out a new expedition, with prominent learnings and a remarkable TO-DO list that you can apply to your new journey.

Never sit back feeling dejected...... Life is made of numerous opportunities and journeys!

Just Keep at it!

Every milestone

you covered

added a

layer of strength

& wisdom,

never forget

this

The Illusion of Money

This chapter has many interesting aspects.

Money is very interesting. After reading much about it I realized, you don't learn the lesson by reading, you need to experience it. Period!

Money is something which will keep running away from you the more you run after it in the pursuit of happiness or the illusion of it.

Take this as a fact, though you will experience it yourself at every step, that **money and happiness are vastly unrelated**.

There was a time I hardly had a decent place to stay and even arranging for two square meals in a day was an ardent task!........ Not because I had less money but because I didn't have any!

money

&

happiness

are

vastly

unrelated

After working for almost twelve hours daily, I had to cook food for myself, eat it, wash dishes and sleep for few hours and repeat the same the next day, day after day, all of this when I was at the far end but still in my teens.

The image of money was always blurry and I had no misconceptions that someone will save me someday!

"No one is coming to Save you; you have to Save yourself."

I had this recurring dream, yes, I had one, even in adversity, that one day I will have a good life partner, of my choice, a child and a home of my own, and a Car. And I will be happy and content.

This was all of it, this was my dream, just to reach the basic level of living, out of the grueling & unforgiving turmoil of survival!

Every cell in my body used to yearn for achieving this dream. I was infected with darkness and this little ray of Hope was my only savior.

And as 'The SECRET' states the Law of Attraction comes into play when you want something bad enough, thinking about it day in and day out, living it daily in your mind.

I eventually married a girl I wanted to, have a daughter, whom I love so much and I have a house and a car.

No one

is coming

to

Save you;

you have

to

Save yourself

Out of all this, my happiness is related to my wife and my daughter. If you list all the material things I have and add my child's name and partners name, every time I will look at the material things normally but feel happy to see their names.

Money is very important and when you buy something that you desire, you feel happy, however, the feeling is momentary, temporary and loses its sheen at a greater velocity than the sheen on the product itself!

I will harp on it a bit longer.

[you might want to take a chocolate & chips break here!]

Suppose you buy a Ferrari one day; you will feel ecstatic. You will flaunt it, people will appreciate you, and a few drives later you will not even look at it, **it will become just another thing!**

"But then again, now I want a different Car, which will make me happy."

However, your achievements, what made you buy them in the first place, will always bring a smile to your face, **"Yes! I did it."**

A man had millions of Dollars but his wife didn't love him, his child hated him and he was always depressed due to this.

Though all this while he was staying in a palatial villa, bathed in an infinity pool, had a string of chefs at his beck

& call who prepared numerous delicacies every day.

Travelled in a Ferrari to work.

Another man had very little money, had a loving wife, who cared for him, was always by his side in all circumstances, had a lovely child who liked to spend time with him.

The man always remained happy!

You decide what is better, you decide what life you want for yourself.

Money will only serve its purpose; it will not give happiness.

Aspire for a loving family with friends to be on your side.

Money is a desirable dream and achievable too but if you run after it, you will miss all the good things in life which you experience with or without money. The experience of exploring a new place, even if it's at a walkable distance, dipping your biscuit in that famous tea stall at the roadside, a friend by your side to share all the secrets, to share endless laughter directed at anything and everything!

The ideal is to have money and a happy family. You must strive for it. But the latter is a must, no compromise on it!

"Yes! I did it."

You will have to work at it though by showing genuine care and affection.

You will be happy and earning money or wealth would seem worth the while!

What good is all the money in the world if you don't have people who love you, by your side, you can spend it with.

We come to an interesting part of this chapter now.

Tell me, what will you do if you had all the money in the world or all that your heart desires or your mind can conceive as sufficient!

 I'll take a guess!

Allow me please.

Thankyou.

Here goes.

You will

*Eat a breakfast with 20 amazing dishes.

*Eat a lunch with 30 delicious dishes

*Eat dinner with 20 aromatic delicacies.

*Go to the shopping plaza daily and buy all the world-famous brand attire, gadgets, scandals, shoes, bags, accessories.

Tool kit for Children

*Buy exclusive furniture and keep changing it daily.

*Buy Cars every week.

*Book tickets for all the exotic places in the world and travel daily.

*Watch your favorite movies every day.

*Will repeat all of this forever.

You will do all of this until you realize, real soon, that all of this holds some satisfaction for only a few days!

You will get so awfully disgusted with all this "stuff" that you will want to give it up, all of it, and become a recluse, or if that is too much then at least will start craving for the life you were leading, one of simplicity, limited needs, and few desires, ones you were aspiring to achieve, and in your aspiration, was happy, to walk on that journey, to pursue that goal.

It is not hard to understand that you need a balanced breakfast, a simple, less spicy lunch, and a bit of dinner, no matter how much money you earn.

You can only travel as much, or else your body will retaliate and, your soul will become restless.

You can buy a limited set of clothes and accessories and think of them as just essentials.

The more you clutter your home and surroundings with things, mostly useless after a while, the more your mind will be cluttered.

Less is More, always.

You will get immense happiness if you will help someone in need, or some people or some community. You will be at peace.

You will be Happy if you exercise and meditate and look within, rather than look without.

Until the Illusion of Money is alive you will be happier than when you actually have it.

There will be no emotion then, when you will have money.

Remember to practice being humbler.

Remember to practice being more polite once you have it.

Remember to practice being more generous when you have it.

Less

is

More,

Always

Remember, that once you become rich, you will be observed more, in all these aspects.

Yes, you are right you will need to practice them, if you don't already have these virtues.

With practice you can achieve all of this.

It will become a part of you.

Until the

Illusion of

Money is alive

you will

be

happier than

when you actually

have it

The Illusion of Fame

When we are young we look at celebrities, designers, Industrialists and immediately develop a liking towards them due to their achievements, wealth, sports cars, palatial houses, lifestyle.

We follow them on social media and spend hours looking at their lifestyle, attire, behavior and mannerisms.

We are drawn towards their "*Good*" lives and know that we will also become that someday.

We just know it.

We ignore, however, their struggles and turmoil and fierce determination, and perseverance to reach there! Even the ones we presume to have been born with a silver spoon have lived through a nightmare

to live up to the expectations of matching up with their legacy.

We fail to see this.

Fame thus causes an Illusion that just chews into our precious time.

Also, we must know that what they show on the exterior, confidence, charisma, and constant smile, might just be superficial. They have to be in the eye of the media, fans, public scrutiny almost all of their waking hours, and hence the eye-catching, polished outward mantle.

Even they have numerous issues, problems, and their own devils which reside inside their minds.

We talked about this in the earlier chapter "*The Illusion of Money*".

One more aspect of Success we must ponder upon.

Their achievement of what they could build gives them happiness and keeps them going.

Yes, even if they have to exert themselves and push themselves many times. But it's true that their arduous journey to reach where they are must have made them very strong and instilled an unshakable belief that goals can be achieved if one keeps at it.

The journey has to be undertaken; milestones have to be crossed. And while you are walking you never know what surprises are in store for you!

Fame thus

causes an

Illusion

which just

chews

into

our precious

time

For living their best life

The journey has to be undertaken though.

Don't ever let yourself convince you that fame will come easily.

Don't ever be in the illusion of fame just because it looks easy.

Trust me, what looks easy, and simple would be the hardest to achieve.

There is nothing that is called "by default". It is only "by design".

You need to wear your shoes, tie the laces strong and begin the journey, and fall, and fall, but never turn back.

Burn your bridges.

The journey

has

to

be

undertaken

though

Don't give yourself excuses to return. Carry "Inspiration" in a bottle to deal with disgust & despair.

Disgust & Despair will be your two very good friends, they will keep you going.

The more you see of these two, the more you will be sure that you are getting nearer to your glory.

I will explain how.

When you start scaling the steep mountain, initially it is all convenient, happy, easy, inspirational, and motivational. You exhume confidence and self-belief.

As the climb gets tougher, all the above "friends" start leaving you one by one.

Whom are you left with?

Yes, that's right.

Your two friends, Disgust & Despair.

They will remind you of the troubles, obstacles, the immense pain.

And in all of this, you will see your glory and push yourself.

Disgust & Despair

will be

your

two

very good friends,

they

will

keep

you going

You will know that it's going be the most painful at the other end of our journey, when the dream is in sight, it will break you, but you will keep at it.

Remember your two friends.

Don't lose them.

There are famous movie stars who didn't have any background, education in acting, but they got noticed by someone, somewhere, at a place where they were coincidentally present. That happened by chance.

Next are those who took education to sharpen their acting skills but struggled for years until someone noticed them and finally, they got to prove themselves and are now famous.

There are those who had a legacy, parents in movies, day-in-day-out part of the stardom and so they got a chance rather easily.

Again, in spite of this convenience, while we may think that since they were born with a silver spoon, they will be successful, in many cases, these people have failed in their first movie or after the first one which was hugely successful.

They just couldn't adapt or they lacked the talent or the passion or were just plain misfits!

Hence, even if someone leads you to the treasure location, you will have to do the digging yourself!

To get the Fame you have to keep digging and keep the faith.

even if someone

leads you

to

the

treasure location,

you will have

to do the digging

yourself

Style & Substance

While style can be an important aspect of your life, in how you move and make an impression on others, it can become like a honey dipped pie without the honey!

There are few thoughts I will share.

Style can be of two kinds. One which is natural. "Look at the way he speaks, or, the way she uses hand gestures while talking, or, see how his left brow raises. These and many more can be inherent, that is to say, coming from the womb.

Another kind can be, the acquired one, where you have worked consciously on certain aspects. Like hairstyle, the way you walk, speak or even smile. All this can be learned and practiced.

Important to add that the ones, carefully thought through, to improve one's persona, adds vastly to the journey towards success. So, it is very useful.

Having said that, there is another aspect that can supersede this advantage in more than one way. Substance. It is your soul. Core. It is the difference when people remember that "One person" out of hundreds!

It is something that can be felt, like a light from an enlightened person. Substance is what fills our shallow being. If we go literally by the term 'Substance' it means something which fills up. Some mass or volume. It is voluminous! Something which can fill an empty vessel.

Though it is also natural but can be acquired as well, consistently practicing a few traits, diligently, and mostly by doing certain things until they become an essential part of your being.

Substance is directly related to Integrity, ethics, tolerance, generosity, thoughtfulness, and reflection.

We never ever say, "Look at this gangster or This criminal has so much substance in him", we don't

because he hasn't any.

He is shallow and vain. The show of Style & Substance he displays is only attributed to his illusion of

power and is completely shallow.

Important to note that Substance without Style can still

lead a person to the height of his or her dreams and make them stay there but only *Style without Substance* will make them fall sooner than later, even if they reach there somehow!

The best combination is to have both Style & Substance! Again, can be acquired with effort & time.

[take a break now, eat a burger maybe, or listen to some music, see you soon]

Style without Substance

will make

them

fall

sooner than later,

even if they

reach there

somehow!

The real world

I know you are fond of movies and like the adventure, drama, suspense, emotions portrayed in them.

You like happy endings and shed happy tears and feel sad when endings are sad and shed tears of pain.

For those few hours you are truly a part of the film.

You live another life than your actual life.

What's the difference? Isn't it all the same?

You might ask, isn't all of this happening in my life too?

Today it's all peaceful and tomorrow suddenly brings unwanted excitement.

Or

Today it feels gloomy, due to no reason at all, probably just the weather, but tomorrow it's all sunshine and happiness!

Like the gloom never happened.

Yes.

You will move on or will learn to do so.

[This is an exciting & essential chapter so you might want to keep this book aside for a while,

I say, just prepare for this chapter, grab a chocolate drink if you can……….. see you soon]

Ok.

So, you are back.

Don't like milk? Some potato wafers maybe? No?

Am I beating about the bush? Maybe, I also need a change in my writing and interaction with you.

Don't you think?

No?

Huh!

No issues, let's move on anyways…….

So, I am talking about The Real World!

How is it different from your present world?

We must find out.

Until now you have been in a covered, secure and shielded environment.

Tool kit for Children

How?

You are in your comfort zone with your family taking care of you in many ways, even though you have become independent now in a few of your tasks, and if you have entered your teenage then you seek privacy too, sometimes a lot of it.

However, you are still protected.

You have to go to school, in a protected transport system, with a teacher to accompany you. School again is shielded, and you come back home.

In the evenings you probably go to see your friends, in the same colony or society.

You are touching the borders of the main road, at the most, that too either you are accompanied or just hurry through that patch.

You are not worrying about your food or clothes or where to live at this moment.

You don't need to. That's how it is.

You only need to study, develop your hobbies, acquire new skills, chat with friends, learn to cook, and pick up a sport.

This is your life and your present.

But in all of this, you are aware of another kind of life which is so different from the present one.

How are you aware?

You see it everywhere, in your own house, your parents, their lives, their career, their entire scenario.

At this stage, you will distinctly observe that your parents have begun to prepare you for the transition. It happens smoothly.

Or rather it should.

And hence all this writing.

The time is approaching when sooner rather than later you will step out of the house alone, unshielded.

There is no bus to college, no teacher to accompany.

Change is even bigger if your college is in a city or country other than your current home!

But nothing to worry about, you will be just fine!

We, humans, are equipped with a "Survival kit". It develops with time and comes out in need. It becomes our shield for the rest of our lives.

Very important, this Survival kit.

We must protect it at all costs.

You are

not worrying

about your food

or

clothes

or

where to live at this mo-
ment

I will go into details please.

I must. For your sake.

"Survival kit" is an invisible bag which is attached to us even before we are born, in our mother's womb.

While all these years, your parents, relatives, grandparents, friends, and teachers have been with you, you are not in much need of the Survival kit.

But at the opportune time, it activates on its own and covers you!

Now that's a relief, isn't it?

So, you might ask.

Then why do I need to read all of this?

The Survival kit will shield me, anyways, right?

Right.

Here is the thing.

You are about to set foot in a magnificent landscape.

It has jungles, lakes, mountains, gorges, valleys, desserts, isolated spots, lush green grounds, and waterfalls.

The Survival kit

will

shield

me,

anyways

right?

And before you, many people have entered the place and are now on their own.

Some will discover lakes and waterfalls, some will discover desserts and canyons, some will reach the lush green grounds and will not want to move further while others will want to see all the vivid pastures and views that life has to offer.

Now picture this, you enter knowing all of this and are excited and joyous. You should be.

However, no one has sat you down and made you aware of the perils!

Perils?

But…….?

Remember there is a price to be paid.

Where there is day and, sunshine, there is also night and darkness.

You need to know that you should have a torch and batteries for the dark.

At least this much you ought to know.

Where there
is day, sunshine,
there is
also,
night and
darkness

It's not that without this knowledge you will not find it out, you will, but after spending a few nights in darkness, skeptical, nervous and doubting the future, this experience, has caught you unawares.

And so, you should know at least some part of it.

Only the part which tells you how to use the Survival kit!

The kit will shield you but you have to use it prudently, to its potential, and know which tools to use when and which weapon to use for which fight.

Sometimes you don't have to cross the entire river to know how deep it will be or what dangers there might be. You enter the river and feel the current. You look at the color of the water and know how deep it can be.

This is how I discovered a few tools from the Survival kit, but since no one told me about them before, an enormous time was lost just in the discovery.

Time, I could have used in scaling the mountain or crossing the river.

So, learn about few of the tools and discover some on your own.

Tool kit for Children

First lesson is on Happiness.

Tie this lesson in a knot and put it safely in the insides of your Survival Kit.

"Do not look for your Happiness in others, it was inside you and will be there always."

You will face disappointment if you look for it in others, thus creating a monster called "Slimy Expectation Lizard!".

With this, I move to your first impression of the world, which will be immediately affected by "Humans".

"Humans"

They will be everywhere, almost all the time.

Strangers at first, then, known to you.

"Humans"

Do not

look for

your Happiness in others,

it was inside you

and will be

there

always

Tool kit for Children

Vast seas of Humans from all kinds of religions, caste, age, size.

Their biases, prejudices, insecurities, superficial personas.

From the day one you will come across these and also the ones who come across as genuine, polite, and charming.

And here is the lesson.

Never judge the book by its cover.

Never judge a human by his or her charm, status, or even if he seems superficial initially.

Only with time, you will know the real person and the values that person holds.

But don't rush to form your opinion, as I am sure you would not want others to form an opinion about you just by looking at you.

Although you can, but then we are here to use the Tool Kit remember?

Let's go through this for our learning.

Never judge

the

book

by

its

cover

Tool kit for Children

Generally speaking, when you are receiving knowledge, any kind, it is important, almost crucial to respect it, and hold it within you.

Even if you think that it is of very less use to you, still preserve it, in your heart. One day it might come in handy!

Don't let your guard down.

We all have our weaknesses and it might be best to keep them under cover unless you decide to reveal them to a person you trust.

And Trust is not built in a day just like Rome wasn't.

It takes certain instances, gestures, and deeds to build trust.

All said and done, trust will be the binding adhesive in any relationship. It is the foundation. Like the foundation of a building.

Without it, it will fall.

It's also not important to try and build trust with everyone.

There will be people at your workplace with whom you will just have a matter-of-fact relationship Work-related only. There, being professional is extremely important and wise too.

Then your colleagues turned friends, like in school or college. They will be your support initially, in the new environment.

However, initially, you have to establish yourself in the workplace as someone who is dependable. So be there, give your time and effort ,and create your space.

It will be very tough in the beginning but if you put your head and heart into it, you will feel better and much in control.

Important to note that there will be people who would want to get close to you but you need to be cautious as to where to draw the line!

Trust me, I am saying this for a female and a male as well. Remember, I said in the beginning? There are all kinds of "Humans" in this world!

Ones you can't even imagine as yet.

But you will find out.

Amongst all of them, be self-contained, self-assured, and remain fiercely independent!

You must learn to love your company.

To be with you.

Then there will be strangers.

Like the ones on the road, on a train, Cab drivers' shopkeepers, and in offices.

This species you don't know and will not like to know.

Tool kit for Children

However, they will be there all the time.

Remain calm, remain yourself and most of all remain alert!

Why alert?

Why aware?

To be safe & secure.

Since we don't know them, we don't trust them.

We don't distrust them but don't trust them either.

So, let's keep away and be alert.

You must

learn

to

love

your

company

Tool kit for Children

I would very logically suggest driving your own vehicle to work or elsewhere as much as you can, for both male or female, but especially for a female.

This way you can remain independent, be in control, reach where you want to with ease, and can go where you want to go!

No dependence.

Although at times you would have to call a cab, then be vigilant.

There are tools you can activate here as well, like GPS notifications to your family, looking for suspicious signs, and avoiding late hours.

Taking precautions is not harmful when they can lead us to safety.

Our dreams depend on our well-being and health, Period!

No discussions on this.

We can explore the lush green grounds, the waterfalls, canyons, and rivers of life, be where ever we want to be, and do whatever we want to, but only if we are taking care of ourselves at all times.

Think about this.

You learn to drive a car.

You are cautious on the first day of training, on the second day, the tenth day, the twentieth day and then one day you know how to drive.

So now you take your car out on your own, you are cautious still.

First few days you drive on an almost uninhabited road, then you gain confidence and you drive in a bit of traffic and then finally start going out on main roads where there is a full flow of vehicles, honking, speeding, and then cycles coming in front of you without any warning, cows sitting gleefully in the middle, buses swerving on your side carelessly!

What do you do, just because now you are confident in driving, you stop being cautious?

You will drop your guard? No!

That will be being overconfident. Which is fatal.

What do you do, just because now you are confident in driving, you stop being cautious?

You will be cautious for as long as you take the steering in your hand, for the rest of your life.

Likewise, no matter what and where you are, you have to be cautious of your surroundings, people, and situations in life!

Not that you have to be in panic but any unusual sign should not go unnoticed from your end, that's all.

There was this sign in neon which was placed on one of the bents of the road while going to my home town.

"Alert Always Avoids Accident".

It's true & forever relevant.

Through my observation, I would tell you the below.

I have seen people who are very cautious or seem so or people who seem overconfident, or ones who seem extra jovial, these people attract undue and unwanted attention from strangers! And get in trouble or not at all required harassment.

Alert

Always

Avoids

Accident

Their Survival Kit is either not opened by them or not explored or they don't even know whether they have one already!

They will find out the torch in some time, and then it will take a few more days, maybe many, to know the use of it.

Imperative to use the right tools from the Survival Kit at the right place and time.

I am repeating myself; I know, this is the essence of this lesson so I have to, for you, for your betterment.

Think of this as a driving school.

You will still have to take your car out on the road one day, alone.

You will apply the teachings for sure but the road will teach you many things which no school or book can teach you.

All the scenarios cannot be covered

Your tools while driving:

Steering.

Accelerator.

Gear knob.

Brake pedal.

Clutch.

Tool kit for Children

Rear view mirror.

Alertness.

Vigilance.

A 360-degree awareness.

Avoiding calls at all times while driving.

Keeping your eye in front at all times.

Inflated spare wheel.

Lifting jack.

Enough fuel in the tank.

All lights are functional.

This is your survival kit for your car and for good driving.

All of this has to be ensured at all times, every time, forever.

Such is Life.

Your Survival Kit has to be ready at all times.

Enjoy the Drive! Let the cool breeze fill your car.

It's a biased world

Might not be an interesting chapter but an important one, this much I can assure you.

You saw in previous chapters; how essential it is to be aware.

We hear many things daily through social media, different videos, and blogs.

We become aware, even though we might not agree.

The truth remains whether you agree with it or not.

I implore you to accept the reality first, then figure out what to do with it or about it.

And then deal with it.

Manage it.

What is the reality?

The reality is that you are going to face bias and if I could write down the synonyms as well, it would not be an over kill.

Prejudice

Partiality

Unfairness

Favoritism

Yes, these hard-hitting words.

Since you know that I am writing this from my observations, also know that it is also through my own experience, which I have faced at many crucial junctures of my career and life.

So, although this may seem more skewed towards the female gender, even males are affected by it, sometimes more dearly.

What is bias exactly?

Bias is a disproportionate weight in favor of or against an idea or thing, usually in a way that is closed-minded, prejudicial, or unfair. People may develop biases for or against an individual, a group, or a belief. In science and engineering, a bias is a systematic error. Wikipedia.

Synonyms of Bias

Prejudice

Partiality

Unfairness

Favoritism

Yes, these hard-hitting words

I think it is a systematic error in the brains of humans to form such biases.

Don't you feel the same way?

Isn't it prudent to approach a person basis of his or her credentials or intelligence or social standing?

Instead of color, race, or gender?

It should be but it's not.

So now we have a situation at hand and one which needs to be dealt with, once and for all.

Preparation is good when we know that something is permanent and will not go away.

Let's discuss gender bias first.

This will hit you like a Tsunami initially and rightly so, as this is the mother of all biases.

Read this with intent now. Few ground realities.

A female has been considered weak for centuries.

She has been thought of as an inferior being. Inferior to the male gender.

The slight weakness in physical strength has been also been taken as a default weakness in mental strength.

By doing so, the male gender has brought shame and disgust to itself, and with ignorance, he covers all of this cheap propaganda.

There is another problem.

Since males have always 'thought' of themselves as superior beings, they get utterly uncomfortable in the company of a female who has a better standing than them; social, financial, and educational.

In this situation, they will try out various ways to impress the female or even make advances, in order to again suppress the female.

They will also cross boundaries at times, not all, but the frivolous ones, to vomit out unnecessary anecdotes or irrelevant data just to show themselves as better in knowledge. Unfortunately, by doing so they will again prove that they are so vain.

The slight weakness

in physical strength

has also been taken

as a

default weakness

in

mental strength

In a situation where a female is part of growth with all other members as males, including the boss, she will always find herself cornered and challenged for her entity, her way of working, the way she talks, eats and so and so forth.

Not because she had any of these issues in the first place, but because even the boss is a male and he is also a stereotype!

Hence, functioning as per the herd or sheep mentality, all the group members will side with the boss and the boss will outcaste the female thus contradicting the very basis of leadership.

'Take everyone along, appreciate virtues, build on failures, celebrate successes, know everyone's strengths, and work on weaknesses.' The core of leadership.

While I have seen and even been part of many groups where the boss is only concerned about the efficiency and effectiveness of an employee and keeps everyone focused in this direction, never ever hinting or being a part of any bias. You must believe me that in all such groups, the females outperformed and outshined almost all male members!

Now, what should you think about this.

'Females are superior'?

No.

Don't get into this trap.

Otherwise, again you will now begin to indulge in the game of bias, the one which you felt unjust in the first place.

I would like to draw your attention now to a very crucial aspect.

All this changes very quickly if you *stop playing the part of the victim.*

You go to the workplace as a very neutral person, not looking for any sympathy. Not being apologetic for being a female. {females are conditioned to indulge in self-pity and apology and thus display the same persona}. Not being inferior or superior to anyone, male or female.

Not hating or liking the male gender.

stop

playing

the part

of

the

victim

You will be surprised that while male members will begin with their usual act of superiority, very   soon they will also become neutral with you and everything will change.

So, you, see? The key to this lock, the medicine for this disease will be in your hands all the time. Just use it.

Caution: Do not become this revenge-seeking, oppressed person, out to kill!

 Do not listen to the devil or people who are devils reincarnate, who brainwash vulnerable people into their criminal pattern of thinking. Remember, that there are exceptional, generous, loving, humble people in this world whom you would like to talk to, and befriend. And why not?

Don't miss an opportunity to meet wonderful people, by forming biases!

✱※✳☼❈✻

Be neutral.

At the workplace, if you manage to reach a higher position, like a Head of the department or a business head, you will, by default, surpass any or every trace of bias. But as spring gives us new flowers, different situations will bring another set of biases, so think of it as a part of life and deal with it.

Be

Neutral

Will harp on it a bit more and then we move on to another interesting topic.

You know how fire spreads right? Like, really spreads? By the strong winds. And by heat.

Without wind and heat, there will be no fire. Heat kindles the fire, wind spreads it.

Do not discuss oppression on yourself and all of the female gender, do not indulge in gossip, demeaning males and how they do injustice, do not start the grapevine or be a part of it and automatically you will see that the fire, which did start, never spread.

Put your focus on achieving and not on discussing biases, and very soon you will see any such person or talk disappearing.

Just put off the smoke before it turns into a raging fire.

Treat a person as they are meant to be treated, and don't take any ill-treatment from anyone as well.

I have spoken about bias so that you know what is in fashion. Do your own thing though.

Do not let this affect you and come in the way of your journey. This will form a part of many small pebbles which come on your path!

Tool kit for Children

Who on earth stops and ends the journey or gives in because of these pebbles? Only those who let the pebbles appear bigger than themselves.

✳ ❋ ✳ ❂ ❋ ❋

Interestingly the biases which a male can face can show a different reality.

The female boss can be biased towards female employees and hence be biased against a male. So now the male will be in the arena as the female was. And since he was always conditioned to be superior, he falls from grace and has nowhere to go! The female members of his group and his boss will take him down like hounds take down a meek deer. They will take revenge on him for all the atrocities that males have showered upon women in the many centuries gone by!

All their biases will sprout against this poor, little, harmless soul.

Humor aside, only a sensible female of this group can, in a subtle manner, make things neutral, one who will know that even a male is also a human and has to be treated as one.

In the absence of any such women, either the man should relent or run with both hands up in the air. It is not cowardly to avoid a place, situation or people who oppress and if you are losing strength to hold on.

For living their best life

You are as good as you think you are and not as much as any other person tells you.

Time for a break now and some chocolate shake.

Come back though my dear.

You are

as good as

you think

you are

and not

as much as

any other

person tells you

I look forward…….

to show you the light!

Do the Right thing- & fall

Always remember, there is only one "RIGHT" and not different versions of it, and it cannot be twisted as per our own definitions.

I know various people who have various versions of what is True and what is Right.

They are disillusioned people and live in a smog, very thick, one which has blocked their vision. What

is right as per them, is right. Period!

They are the darkness, who makes us value the light.

And may you remain in Light.

And know Right from Wrong.

If only for the above line, you will lead a fulfilling life, not happy always, but fulfilling and content.

When you step out, you will see how nine persons will wrong the tenth person who was right.

You should know that even a hundred or a thousand people cannot justify the wrong. So even if you're the only one standing, and if everyone leaves you, remember, to hold on to the truth and be true to yourself. This will be a gift from you to yourself.

It will be easier and faster to reach to the top by indulging in the wrong but it will be difficult to stay there as your foundation will be built on wrongful acts.

So why go there in the first place?

Take the right path even if it takes longer.

You were doing all this in the first place for your happiness and peace. Both of these are directly in proportion to being righteous.

Remember? We discussed earlier that money does not provide any happiness? Only a temporary satisfaction?

And no amount of money can fulfill a person's greed.

No amount.

It's a bottomless bucket. Many people consume themselves in trying to fill it but lose their lives in the process. Magic is created with happiness, with a heart filled with love. Love for yourself and what you do.

Take

the

right path

even if

it

takes

longer

When you look in that mirror, you should be proud of what you see.

A warrior confronts his/her enemy, uses tactics, hones his/her skills, remains calm and wins in the end or at least gives his/her best, and doesn't cut corners.

I will not beat around the bush.

There will be temptations throughout.

Don't you like shortcuts?

I Do.

But I like the shortcuts which make me reach somewhere in less time or if I can avoid traffic on the road.

Or if I am tired and alone and don't have the strength to prepare my food, then I can take a shortcut and just eat a sandwich. But not when I am explaining all of this to you. I am doing this honestly.

So that it adds value to your life.

I could have not written this at all and taken a session of an hour with you instead. But that was not me.

I will do a task with complete dedication and that makes me happy.

Even with you, there will be many such occasions where there will be a lure to take a shortcut.

Tool kit for Children

Ask yourself.

Is it for making a sandwich or is it to do with my dream or my life?

There is a difference, clearly.

Know the difference.

Go all out and all the way and beyond if it's a matter of reaching your goal and if it makes you reach a milestone, if not the goal.

Show your passion and zeal.

A person has to necessarily live while she or he is alive.

You must seize the moment and dissolve in it completely.

 I promise if you do that, even after working twenty hours at a stretch you will not feel tired.

Why?

Because you were totally in it, with complete passion.

So, no shortcuts.

I know this sandwich discussion has tickled your stomach so go and take that sandwich shortcut break.

Is it

for making

a sandwich

or

is it

to

do with

my dream?

You must

seize

the moment

and

dissolve in it

completely

Another kind of temptation, which will keep you away from your goal, or rather the happiness of reaching there.

It's financial temptation.

While you will hold certain key positions in your job, there would be a possibility that people might extend financial favors to you to enroll them in your company, or pass that tender etc. They will offer you money which will tempt you because it will be much higher than what the company is giving you.

It's called easy money; it easily kills your soul.

You will no longer look in the mirror and say 'Yes, I did it'.

You will no longer be proud of yourself as a human being.

You cheated on your company and the trust they put in you and gave you a responsible job.

You put the credibility of your position and the company at stake and the company no longer will be considered ethical because word will be out soon that people here receive bribes.

And then the inevitable, of getting caught, and being investigated.

Its

called

easy money;

it easily

kills

your

soul

The list is long and infuriating.

Never go that way.

That path is not for you.

Always follow the right path even if it has those pebbles and even if you are bare feet.

Do the right thing & fall.

But always do the right thing.

There is no other way.

swim like selfish

Yes you must.

For your own sake.

Being selfish is not just the best way to live, but the only way.

Again, you get to choose. After all, it's your life.

But know this perspective, for you, for your life.

You know, I am writing all of this so that you can imbibe a few, or all good things from here, maybe immediately, maybe after a while, or later.

Or maybe when you need it.

Sometimes you might want to take this as a medicine when you are in pain.

Being selfish

is not

just the

best way

to live,

but the

only way

Either way, the question is, why am I doing all this at all?

For you?

No.

Do get this, I am doing this for myself. My own self.

Why?

Because I am selfish. Period!

Doing this will make me happy.

If tomorrow you get successful, I will be happy.

If you get independent and content, it will make me happy.

I am selfish. I am sorry.

✱✺✻✪❄✷

There are two reasons why we do something.

Either for someone else or for ourselves.

That's what we have been told.

In all of it though whatever we do is only for ourselves.

Now the perspective.

When I say I am doing this for you, I confuse you and I further confuse the act of doing or giving.

One, I am doing a favor to you.

I am Selfish, I am Sorry

Once I do a favor, I want a favor in return.

So, I raise expectations.

I start living with these expectations.

I am constantly thinking of how I can take back the favor.

Now, due to some turn in events, I want something and because I did this favor to you already, I think it's my right to ask from you, and you cannot refuse.

You refuse though.

In all honesty, you didn't have the capacity or capability to fulfill my demand.

This agitates me and I, either get furious or break with you.

'How can he refuse me?'.

'When he needed me, I was there!'.

I would become unreasonable.

I carry this burden now in my heart and breed resentment.

And I keep doing this all my life.

Another perspective.

Being selfish.

I do something for you, but for my own sake.

I do it because I want to and I could.

I do not expect anything in return.

Even if I go to you tomorrow for something and you cannot do it, I remain even and understand.

Why?

Because I am selfish. I do not put my peace and happiness on the line for no one or anything. Simple.

There are thousands of ways I can compromise my happiness.

Or.

There will be hundreds of reasons that life anyways gives all of us, in the form of adversities, where we would find it difficult to stay afloat, to remain happy.

So, why should I deliberately attract unhappiness by going off track?

I will stay clear of self-inflicting wounds.

The pebbles on my path are enough to do that.

So be selfish.

You are in the office and a part of a five people team.

Your boss offers to make a presentation. What would you do?

Tool kit for Children

Sneak behind others?

I know why. And I understand.

You already have so much work. Your boss doesn't empathize, doesn't tweak the deadlines at all and you are already working long hours!

And another burden of a presentation?

God no!

Remember being selfish?

A 'selfish' will grab the offer, with both fins and digest it before anyone else even blinks!

Yes, you read it right!

Why?

Because the selfish person loves herself and was always waiting for this.

An opportunity, to break away from the herd, to finally become the smart wolf it was, but was hiding all this while, under the skin of a sheep!

For a selfish person this opportunity will push her towards the next milestone faster than others.

So, she will make the presentation during the night, will not sleep, will not complaint and present it. And because she loves herself, she will give it her best shot.

So, why should I deliberately attract unhappiness by going off track?

And before she knows it, her boss will start giving her more responsibilities and before long she will be ready for the next promotion.

All this is because she keeps herself ahead of others and is ready to climb the steps.

I was discussing this with you today, so I write it here as well.

Everyone wants to climb the steps to success, but most just climb down after taking a few. Climbing steps takes a lot of effort, your legs hurt, your feet revolt, you feel vertigo after a while, you are out of your comfort zone! There are no side rails to hold on to.

The higher you go, the lonelier you feel, and then? You climb down! To the safety of mediocrity!

A selfish person doesn't do that.

She will deliberately break her chains of comfort and climb toward her freedom.

Freedom from taking directions, freedom from living a sub-optimal life.

So, she is selfish.

Before you ask, this selfishness is not mean spendthrift rift or aloof. In fact, this one is very friendly, very generous, very humble, very ethical, and genuine.

All this is because she is selfish. If she is good and generous then she will be a good person, and people will revere her, respect her, be inspired by and follow her.

She will not let herself down by being mean or anarchic! A selfish person never lets herself down.

She is, on the contrary, a team player, a leader, and a visionary.

She will be a guide, a mentor to hundreds of people, waiting to climb the steps but not able to see the light, not able to locate your hand due to the mist up there!

Yes, mist, at that level, you will not be visible, you will be high up.

The higher you go, the

lonelier

you feel,

and then?

You climb down!

To the safety of

mediocrity!

Read the signs, grab that presentation, take up that event, sign for being a volunteer and never, ever fret for the extra work!

Take a pick, extra work for life or for the moment.

Think about yourself.

Yes mist,

at that level,

you will not

be visible,

you will be

high up

It's your life.

So, what do you want to be?

Selfish?

Yes, you must swim like selfish.

Dream big-be specific

There is a thing with dreams, they come true.

Most humans are unaware of this simple truth. They keep dreaming about failure and poverty and mediocrity, and guess what? their dreams come true.

That's all they dream about.

Then there are people who are always engrossed in controversies as that's what is in their minds always, so their dreams come true.

There are others who dream of a good life but are not specific. Their definition is incomplete with various clauses and conditions.

They are afraid to dream big and bigger. They think they won't be happy and remain feeling inferior.

What you ask is what you get.

What will you strive for if you don't even have a dream which is fulfilling and inspiring?

One that sees you through in darkness and takes you towards the light.

A dream never weakens in darkness, it's you who gets weak and loses hope, and stops believing in yourself and in your dream.

The key is to hold on to it as if your life depended on it. Water it, like you do to your plants, feed it with fertilizers, with positive thoughts.

Think of your dream every day. Most of all be specific.

There is a difference between day dreaming and dreaming. Daydream gets over by night but the dream remains with you. It is your food for the soul and for your heart. You are emotional about it.

What will
you strive
for if you
don't even
have a dream
which is
fulfilling
and inspiring?

They say *'be careful about what you wish for, as one day it might come true'*.

If you understand the importance of this above line, you will not play with it. You will be careful.

You want to become a CEO of a big company.

That's specific.

That's great.

That's an inspiring landmark.

So, what do you do?

You start following the CEOs of the world and take inspiration.

You start to learn the directions, read the map, and understand various milestones on the way.

You begin to know the pitfalls of the journey, the bumps, the treacherous terrains, and also the green pastures, which will come, ahead of the journey, not right away.

So, you start to prepare.

But all along you do not forget the destination.

That will keep you passionate and energetic.

You start with a specific dream.

'Now the thing about dreams.'

It doesn't owe you anything, you are not

doing any favors.

You are doing it because of your happiness.

Remember, you are selfish.

The moment you let go, falling weak, because of the difficulties, the dream goes away!

It was never yours.

A dream is such, that it never lets you sleep; you are always walking. It doesn't make you weak, it makes you stronger.

So, go all out and give it your best shot.

And the pitfall?

Even before your mind stops you, there will be people around you, ready to pull you down!

And more often than not, out of compassion, they tell you to give up.

Take your own decision and stand up for yourself. If you fail trying, it was worth it!

Begin again. There is no dearth of dreams.

Dream again. Be specific, again!

Write down your dream in black & white, read it many times and see it coming to life with all the colors of the rainbow!

Protect your dream. It is sacred. Never make fun of it.

That dream is looking up to you to nurture it and make it feel good.

It has to have good company.

Respect it.

It will be with you.

It will be loyal to you.

Remember, it is very sensitive as well. Any sign of distrust or disregard and will just go.

No goodbyes. It is insensitive in that sense.

That dream

is looking

up to you

to nurture it

and

make it

feel

good

When people lose their purpose in life, it is the dream, they are talking about, that they have lost!

The purpose is the dream.

The dream is the purpose.

It's true. Purpose has to be there, or it has to be planted.

That purpose will make you live with enough and more happiness.

That dream, that purpose. It's the same.

Always, at all times, keep at least one dream in your pocket.

Even though it has got the depth to give you the entire universe, it will not take up much space in your pocket.

A pocket with a dream & no money is much better than a pocket with money & no dream!

The moment money finishes, there is a vacuum.

The purpose,

is the

dream.

The dream,

is the

purpose.

But with a dream in his pocket, even a pauper is a prince, with such a bounce in his walk, with a glint in his eyes, with a dance in his feet, and a forever smile on his lips. It will make you envious of him, wanting to let go of all your possessions, just to be in his shoes!

That's the power of a dream.

This world, as we see it, was made by dreamers, ones who were paupers, but felt like princes or princesses.

Nothing could break them.

So, tell me.

Do you have a dream?

Do you have it in your pocket?

What is your dream?

Have you written it down?

Do you carry it with you?

Do you think it's the most valuable possession you have as yet?

Is your answer to the above a No?

A pocket

with a dream

& no money

is much

better than

a pocket with

money &

no dream!

Will you keep one now in your pocket and see your life change around you?

You must.

One life you have, limited time there is, and so many happy dreams. Begin now and blossom.

Your soul is waiting for your dream!

So, tell me.

Do you have a dream?

If yes, know this, you are richer than anyone on this earth. You are wealthy beyond imagination.

A wish for you.

May your pocket be glowing with dreams of the colors of a rainbow, ones which tickle you just by feeling them, looking at them, ones which give that bounce in your walk, and a forever mysterious smile on your lips!

Ones that make onlookers wonder and gasp! 'What's up with this person?'

'Has he lost his nut?'

Lose your nut! Let them think you are crazy!

Because you are.

 You will not be the sheep in the herd!

You will throw that sheepskin, covering you all this while, and let everyone see, you are the wolf!

So, tell me.

What's your dream?

You will

throw that

sheep skin,

covering you

all this while,

and let

everyone see,

you are

the wolf!

Religion–Just be the tenth one

Sensitive topic. Needs to be dealt with sensitively, more importantly, sensibly.

However, more often than not, sense & sensibility stand poles apart and for three valid reasons.

Ignorance. Ignorance. Ignorance.

Yes, just these three reasonable reasons.

Just as the foundation of many notes before this chapter. Remember, Bias? Or the Illusions?

This one tops it all and, in that sense, is also very close to my heart.

✶❋✲✹❋✶

Ignorance.

Ignorance.

Ignorance.

Yes, just these three reasonable reasons

Tool kit for Children

Let's start from the beginning or let's begin from the start!

Normally when you twist something you get to the same point, like the above sentence.

But not religion.

The more you twist it, the more versions of it are created and everyone ends up with their own version, no matter how twisted.

If you understood the 'Do the right thing-& fall' and 'Swim like selfish', you will find this chapter much more meaningful and can be a turning point in your life, if not today, in times to come.

Read this one without bias. First condition.

Read this for a perspective, not for any new version.

This is not my version coming out of a twisted tale. It's much twisted already. Let's not even go there.

Today we will see, what is, as it is, not how it should be, or how it can be.

No twist, no knots. Knots can be naughty! We talked about the 'Right' thing and how people conveniently twist it as per their own 'wrongs' and come up with their own version of the 'Right'.

A question to me.

'Who the hell am I to decide what's right and what's wrong?'

'Maybe I have twisted it as per my version?'

Can these be the two most relevant questions anyone can ask me?

Correct.

I agree.

These are the two questions, in the first place, which started the twisting concept centuries ago, making the nine people banish the tenth one, accusing him to be wrong, whereas in reality, all nine were wrong to the core!

They had asked him these two questions.

He couldn't address them.

But I will. I must.

Read the below and answer the question which follows;

Nine people are driving in the wrong direction, on a road.

One person is driving on the correct side.

The nine people, seeing him coming, start abusing him, showing aggressive gestures, and threatening to beat him!

This tenth person is at the risk of a major accident, at the risk of losing his life!

Tool kit for Children

This one person has to, in order to save his life, take his car off road and let them pass.

Question for you. Who is right and who is wrong?

Correct.

Nine are wrong and the tenth one is right.

Always keep this in mind, just because nine or a hundred, or a thousand, or a million, or an entire community agrees to something, it's not necessary that it's 'Right' and it's your choice, not to follow it!

They all are operating in the 'Sheep mentality Syndrome', a syndrome which threatens to banish them from their herd, their people, and their bunch of like-minded people.

So, they follow the dogma, the accepted, the norm.

I am not asking you to rebel or oppose. No.

You just have to do the 'Right' thing.

Just be the tenth person, that's all.

For God's sake! Just be the tenth person, that's all!

For Allah's sake! Just be the tenth person, that's all!

For Christ's sake! Just be the tenth person, that's all!

For Krishna's sake! Just be the tenth person, that's all!

Just be

the tenth

person,

that's

all

Tool kit for Children

For Guru Nanak's sake! Just be the tenth person, that's all!

For Buddha's sake! Just be the tenth person, that's all!

Just be the tenth person, that's all.

Of course, be on that road, drive that car, but no matter what happens, be that tenth person.

For God's sake, do not become one of the nine people!

Never.

If you do that, then burn this book, and delete the digital print.

I am pushing it. For you.

I am selfish.

I can't see you fall, by doing the 'Wrong'.

There is no glory in it!

All right, so now I am convinced that I have driven home my point well enough, to begin this chapter now!

Yes, to begin this chapter. There was no other way.

I just could not build a beautiful house on a weak foundation, and that takes time.

Now that we are at it, just an off-the-topic, architectural tip: When you actually build your own house, make sure you spend maximum time, effort, and money on the foundation, dig it deep, and use the best concrete and iron and steel. Don't rush. That's the soul and core of your house. For centuries your house will be unscathed. Don't forget, you are selfish, your house has to be strong and beautiful. Not either but both.

In everything you do in life, try to make the core strong first and then work on the beauty.

Remember? Style & Substance?

✻❋✼❂❉✺

Now to our topic, Religion.

When in Rome, do as the Romans do.

No!

Because Romans also need to use their brains sometimes, they cannot blindly follow the usual.

Right?

Right.

Now, you and we, all have been part of some religious community, not by choice, but by default.

So be it.

It's all good and acceptable.

Believe in it, and follow the tradition.

But know what you are following.

Remove the blindfold.

But whatever you do, for God's sake, don't become a tyrant!

No God will agree to it?

Just because God is not scolding you, pulling your ears, or putting you on the right track in person, doesn't mean he is not noticing!

He is noticing and can only empathize with you, as he knows, that you will pay for your sins, just like you will be paid for your good deeds!

Either you pay or get paid. Simple to understand. Right?

Even if you don't know any other thing, you at least know this, it has been spoon-fed to you from the day you were born. Every religion propagates this theory, which is true. It's the truth.

You can choose to ignore it. But the truth still remains, firm.

Be liberal, not a tyrant.

Who is a tyrant? One who only believes in what he says, or does, and punishes everyone who doesn't follow him.

No religion agrees with it.

Every religion has goodness in it, that is the basis of it. The ones at the helm of it, whom we call God, were all exceptional beings, most humble, most generous, most virtuous, most patient, most forgiving, and most righteous. They would give the last morsel of bread to the needy, even if they had not eaten for days. They would follow the path of 'Right' always.

More importantly, they were always the 'tenth' one. Always.

Take refuge in the qualities of God.

Ask yourself.

'When I am following this religion, am I even trying to imbibe any of the virtues in my being?'

'Am I even trying?'

'Am I at least on the 'Right' path?

'Am I truthful to myself and my family and the ones known to me, at least?'

While we have these urges to do great things, we need to start small. It will build up to bigger deeds. Smaller deeds will add up and fill your bucket.

Learn about the deeds of the great one, God.

'Seek and you shall find the truth'.

'Ask and you shall receive'.

Seek.

Ask.

Try.

They are 'God' for a reason

Seek and follow.

But don't let them down just because they are not visible and are not pulling your ears.

Likewise, be liberal. And why not?

You are a human being! Why should you be bound by one way of knowing the truth?

Follow all religions.

They all have goodness and are similar in that sense.

Be neutral.

It's such a huge opportunity to learn about Mohammed, Guru Nanak, Lord Shiva, Jesus Christ, Guru Gobind Singh, and Gautam Buddha. To know why they are revered.

The first thing you will know about them, is, how simple lives they lead, how much sacrifice they did in their lives; how selfless they were!

Know about each one of them. It will be food for your soul.

You will elevate spiritually. The greatest gift you can give to yourself. You will see how it helps you in your journey and how glorious it will become.

Try it!

Believe in their powers. In the hour of your darkness, they will be with you, and show you the light.

It's not philosophy. It's tried and tested.

God appears in many forms. Just believe.

But first, tell God, you are a good person and worthy of his guidance.

Then, in the true sense, you will do good to yourself and to the religion you were born in and born with.

I know numerous people who will bow down before their God, but will not pause a moment before backstabbing others. They will be the ones causing disputes, and indulge in treachery and betrayal for their own mean intentions.

And then pray with all pomp and fervor as per their tradition just to complete the formality!

What good is that?

But first,

tell God,

you are

a

good person

and worthy

of his

guidance

God only asks one thing of you, to be good and true. That's all.

He does not get angry if you did not do this prayer or perform that ritual. He is not mean; he is not human remember?

But he knows when a good person comes in front of him or a bad one comes.

Vibes.

Yes, vibes will tell him. He knows.

Then there are people, who, to show off, will do some charity work, but earn that money through ill means.

Whom are they fooling?

God?

Huh!

He is God, not human.

And then those who say, 'My God is better and best and yours is not', and coax others to join their religion with this logic.

All this has nothing to do with God and his teachings. In fact, it is the opposite of it.

They have twisted pure religion to fulfill their ulterior motives.

But he is watching it all and all of us.

Be neutral.

Be good.

Be liberal.

Be in the good books of God.

Remember, you are selfish.

You cannot let yourself down.

And for God's sake Just be the tenth person, that's all!

Look within-for happiness

This is the final note to you, in this book and also, the most important one.

If this is taken care of, then everything takes care of itself.

If you understand this, you don't even need the previous ten chapters!

You will be good.

I will tell you a story today.

Maybe it will be of interest to you.

Here goes.

There was girl who lived in a town called 'Boringsnoring'.

Her name was 'Couldbehappybut'.

The town was situated atop a beautiful hill, with striking grasslands and crystal-clear ponds!

It was a wonderland.

The dwellers were farmers who grew their own grains and tended their cows, sheep, and poultry.

They were self-sufficient and a very happy lot.

They visited the bustling city once or twice a year for their farming needs or even to sell their extra produce. However, one thing was common.

None of them wanted to live in the city.

Over the years they had noticed growing unrest and unhappiness, seeping into the progressing city!

They would always be smiling on the streets and city people looked at them with amusement or even scorn and think that these small dwellers were superficial or even crazy to smile all the time.

The *Boringsnoring* town people got convinced that despite all the comforts and wealth, the residents were so sad, there was some common plague affecting them.

Couldbehappybut, the girl, had heard stories of the city and she dreamt of being there one day.

She wanted to be away from this boring town with straight-faced, smiling-for-no-reason people!

She used to tell herself that she could be happy but only if she had all the luxuries.

She could be happy but only if she could be away from this dumb farming life.

She could be happy but only if she could make money on her own and lots of it.

These thoughts made her sad and restless and she poured out her angst on unassuming and polite dwellers.

She could not understand their happiness and it irritated her all the more.

So, one evening………

…………. she left the town, for the city.

Couldbehappybut was feeling free and happy and looked forward to the life she wanted.

In her pursuit, she didn't even think to inform her loving parents and how terrible they might feel. She had to find her happiness, which was in the city.

She felt dazed looking at the tall buildings, flashy cars, gadgets, people eating so much variety of food, parks and a thing called a cinema hall!

Somehow *Couldbehappybut* managed a decent job and a decent place to stay. Everything went as usual for a few days until the irritation of *Couldbehappybut* begin to grow. She told herself, she could be happy but only if she had a better job.

She could be happy but only if she had a bigger house.

She could be happy but only if she had more money.

Problem with money – "It is never ENOUGH".

So, she worked harder, longer hours, bought more gadgets, and more things, grew even more bitter, and more irritable, thanks to the perpetual high-pitch frequency of sound in the city.

Sound of cars, people, gadgets, and things.

In some times though…………..

………….. *Couldbehappybut* had a better job, a bigger salary, and the best gadgets!

She played with the gadgets for some time.

Learned from others that these gadgets would need to be flashed, so everyone can see, which will make her happy.

She did that but didn't get happy.

All this began to seem superficial to her.

Couldbehappybut observed that no one was happy!

They only had possessions, they possessed things, houses, cars, and money but it seemed that these things had possessed them!

Stuck in a dilemma, she was once roaming in the park facing her house.

On the corner of a bench, she saw a woman sitting peacefully, with a forever smile on her face.

Problem

with

money

"It is never ENOUGH".

She was alone.

There were children playing near her bench, with all the excitement they had, meaning they were making a deafening noise.

But the woman, instead of getting angry, was watching them with compassion.

After a while, she got up and walked towards a very big luxurious car and as she was about to board *Couldbehappybut* approached her, skeptically.

She just had to. She needed answers.

'Excuse me, can I take your minute please'.

'Sure, go ahead please'.

'I wanted to know the secret of your forever smile'.

'Are you with someone?', asked the woman,

'No, I am alone', came the reply.

'Good, come with me then'.

Hesitantly *Couldbehappybut* got in the car.

'Where are we going?

'You will see shortly, and besides, you want your answer, right?'

Couldbehappybut

observed that

no one was happy!

They only

had

possessions

'And since you asked me the question, let me ask you this, even though I might already know the answer, why aren't you happy?'

'Well, I am from a small town where people do farming. We have fresh air and clean water, but I felt I could be happy but only if I came to the city and had lots of money.

'So, I came here, rather ran way to the city and started earning and now I have all the possessions, which I thought will make happy'.

'But all this has made you sadder', added the woman.

'Yes, true, and I need answers, and then I saw you'.

'And rightly so, when you seek, you find', said the wise woman.

✱✺✳✪❄✹

There were about five people in the room, three of them looked well off while the other two seemed to be on the borderline.

The woman introduced her to all of them.

They all had the forever smile, like the one on the woman's face, like the one on the *Boringsnoring* town people!

The woman took her to a three-seater sofa and sat her down.

'What do you see in these people?'

'They all seemed happy! How?'

'We all are happy because we don't encourage the *Couldbehappybut* monster!'

'You see, happiness, for which you left your peaceful town and came to the city, was never here, it was not even in your town', affirmed the woman.

'It was not in your small job and little money you had, nor in the bigger job and better gadgets you possessed later on', she continued.

'Tomorrow you will fall in love with a handsome man, thinking he will give you happiness and start a life. Well, guess what, he will not be able to give you happiness either!'.

'Why?'

'Because after a few days or months, you will find him normal, when you will get to know him.

And then boring, as he will no longer remain the person who was wooing you and was after you with flowers to impress you, she explained.

'You will again become sad because he will not do all this anymore, no one can'.

'Just like you lost interest in the gadgets, house, and cars, you will lose interest in him, and then you will find another person, another gadget, another house!'.

'But you all are happy and I am not!', interrupted *Couldbehappybut*, holding back tears.

'You are not happy because you are finding it outside of you, whereas it is and will always be within you', revealed the woman.

This hit *Couldbehappybut* like a bullet.

'What? It was inside me all this time? And I have been running around like a fool? I have even pained my parents and all those back there, by running away, unannounced'.

'You see, situations and circumstances and even your stature keep changing in life. There will be lows along with highs. Understand that everything, including our lives, is temporary and ever-changing, holding on to anything, or running after anything while being unhappy in the present moment will never make anyone happy.

'First, be happy with what you have. Tomorrow might not even be there for you, as I said life is temporary for all of us!'.

'You are not happy

because you

are finding it

outside

of you,

whereas it is

and will

always be

within you'

Tool kit for Children

'What good is anything if we die tomorrow, unhappy and even if we live for hundred years? What good it does to live such a long and sad life?', paused the woman, 'only to look for happiness in tomorrow, which never comes'.

'We all have only today and now'.

'Be happy to be alive, to be who you are, for the gifts of God, for nature, for your family, friends. Show genuine love, and be a good person.

'You are here for a limited period of time so, think of yourself as a limited edition!'

'Don't waste yourself, work on yourself'.

'And by all means, aspire. For a better life, even for wealth, but then be happy to receive it and then enjoy it.

'Tomorrow when you lose it all, be happy to know that you are alive and can create it again'.

'But don't treat your family like things, they will not come back, you cannot create them, so stay true to them'.

'Be happy now, this is your moment'.

'There will be times when you get sad, we all do, even I do, but in those times, think of what makes you happy, go to the park, watch a movie, read a book, just let that time pass, distract it!'

'You are
here for a
limited period
of time
so, think of
yourself as a
limited edition!'

'Your sadness will also pass, sooner, if you don't give it importance'.

'Stop treating sadness as your friend, someone who can be with you all the time.'

'Look at it but then ignore it, you will see, it will get weaker and go away'.

 had got her answers.

She knew she will be happy from now on, no matter what. She was happy now.

'You have changed my life, how can I thank you enough', she said to the woman.

'By just being in touch and staying happy', said the woman.

✳ ❋ ✴ ☉ ❄ ❋

'Stop treating

sadness

as your

friend,

someone who

can

be with you

all the time'.

So, here she was, a happier *Couldbehappybut*!

She didn't leave the city, but visited her town, and apologized for her misdeeds.

Now she spent her holidays in the *Boring snoring town*, cheerfully helping with farming, even finding better dealers for their farm produce. Visited every house to ask about their needs, of medicine, toys, and gadgets for the young and brought it all for them on her visits.

She became an ideal for the youth there and everyone loved her.

She went on to make it good professionally and did find a handsome man and settled down.

She felt happy, within.

✱❋✲❂❀❋

And so, I hope you are happy too, and will remain happy.

As we come to the end, I only hope this one thing.

You will not let that sheep skin cover you and let everyone see, you are the wolf!

151

To the wolf.

To the one, who will always be the tenth!

Dear Children,

While this is the end of this book, it's also the beginning of a new outlook for you, even a new life!

The way you will look at your journey and hopefully make it a happier one!

Your happiness & wisdom will be based on the moments you create and cherish. While Facebook, Instagram are all good platforms to connect with friends but moments, real ones, are made outside these, with real friends & family. In the adventures you undertake, in the passion you show while playing in a park, or playing an instrument, singing, creating a new app!

Listen to your heart & remain genuine.

Just Be honest to yourself.

Just Be ethical in all your endeavors.

Just Be happy to live & love.

Just Be!

Tool kit for Children

Finally, few pages are added for you to pen down notes to yourself.

Your learnings from this book will be strengthened once you write them down.

Do this for yourself.

Tool kit for Children

<u>"NOTES TO MYSELF"</u>

Tool kit for Children

<u>"NOTES TO MYSELF"</u>

Tool kit for Children

Tool kit for Children

<u>"NOTES TO MYSELF"</u>

161

Tool kit for Children

<u>"NOTES TO MYSELF"</u>

Tool kit for Children

<u>"NOTES TO MYSELF"</u>

Tool kit for Children

<u>"NOTES TO MYSELF"</u>

9 789356 800038